This book is dedicated to my mother:

"May her soul continue to rest peacefully."

When The Mood Is Right
A Poetry Journey

QUEEN P.

ASA PUBLISHING CORPORATION
AN INNOVATIVE OUTSOURCE BOOK PUBLISHING HYBRID

ASA Publishing Corporation
1285 N. Telegraph Rd., #376, Monroe, Michigan 48162
An Accredited Publishing House with the BBB
www.asapublishingcorporation.com

All Rights Reserved. No part of this publication may be reproduced, stored in a retrieval system or transmitted in any form or by any means electronic, mechanical, photocopying, recording or otherwise, without the prior written permission of the publisher. Author/writer rights to "Freedom of Speech" protected by and with the "1st Amendment" of the Constitution of the United States of America. This is a work of non-fiction poetry. Any resemblance to actual events, locales, person living or deceased that is not related to the author's literacy is entirely coincidental.

With this title/copyright page, the reader is notified that the publisher does not assume, and expressly disclaims any obligation to obtain and/or include any other information other than that provided by the author except with permission. Any belief system, promotional motivations, including but not limited to the use of non-fictional/fictional characters and/or characteristics of this book, are within the boundaries of the author's own creativity in order to reflect the nature and concept of the book.

Any and all vending sales and distribution not permitted without full book cover and this copyright page.

Copyrights©2019 Queen P, All Rights Reserved
Book Title: When The Mood Is Right *A Poetry Journey*
Date Published: 11.09.2019 / Edition 1 *Trade Paperback*
Book ID: ASAPCID2380796
ISBN: 978-1-946746-63-4
Library of Congress Cataloging-in-Publication Data

This book was published in the United States of America.
Great State of Michigan

Table of Contents

Preface 1
Special Thanks 3

Chapter 1 – Motivation and Inspiration 1

Chapter 1 – Motivation and Inspiration 7
- Haiku #1 7
- Why? 11
- Behind the Shadows 13
- New Beginnings 14
- Decisions Decisions 15
- Back in the Groove 16
- Lessons Learned 17
- Speak It Now 18
- Self-Love 19
- On My Way Up 20
- End Chapter Notes 21

Chapter 2 – Universal Feelings 23
- Haiku #2 23
- Tranquility 27

- Pity Party 28
- I Am 29
- Nothing Left to Say 30
- Traces of You 31
- I'm Not Alone 32
- The Great Escape 33
- Anticipation 34
- Free 35
- End of Chapter Notes 36

Chapter 3 – Power of Love 37
- Haiku #3 37
- Next Level 41
- Roller Coaster Ride 42
- When the Mood is Right 43
- Please Wait 44
- Connection 45
- We Are One 46
- Ponder This 47
- Intimacy 48
- Stolen Moment 49
- The Prize 50
- End of Chapter Notes 51

Chapter 4 – Mother and Daughter **53**
- Haiku #4 53
- Mother and Daughter 57
- Dedication to Mother 59
- Worthy 61
- Worthy 61

Meet the Poet **67**

When The Mood Is Right
A Poetry Journey

QUEEN P.

Preface

"Life experiences and events have inspired me to express myself by writing this poetry book. As a novice, my intent is to motivate, uplift and inspire others as well as allowing the reader to feel the desire to just relax and breathe. This is a brand new experience for me. I've taken that leap of faith and I look forward to creating and sharing more of my creative works in the near future. I am an American writer with Caribbean roots, born and raised in New York where I currently reside with my loving family."

Special Thanks

My sincerest and deepest thank you goes to the Almighty One for challenging me to write this book. You were that voice that kept telling me that I must do this. Much gratitude for creating this vision for me.

I must acknowledge Miss Rita, Shelia and Chrystal. You ladies listened to me go on and on about this book. You critiqued, commented and supported me throughout this journey. Thank you for your input and friendship.

My dearest Early, my "Rider" my motivator. You were so consistent with your encouraging words and pushing me to finishing this project. Many thanks; you are awesome. This is just the beginning...

And finally, I must give my thanks, love and gratitude to my family for supporting me from the beginning. Herman, Tiffany, Trevor, Sheryl, Darren and Arya. Your words of encouragement and excitement about my book was overwhelming to me. Thank you for your love and support.

I must extend a special thank you to Miss Renee for taking time out of her busy life to sit with me and help me to pull things together when it came down to finalizing this book. You are loved and appreciated.

Queen P.

Life is not always perfect.

This moment is only temporary.

Mama said there would be days like this,

Just put a bandage on it.

Time heals all wounds . . .

Queen P.

Chapter 1

Motivation and Inspiration

A cup of Green Tea

Essential Oils diffusing

Daily Ritual

Why?

These eyes have seen so many things
to make me question why.
Why can't we form an alliance instead
of turning a blind eye?
Why not extend a helping hand to our

brothers and our sisters?

Why must we be in competition?

Why don't we have more ambition?

Why do we rob, mob and kill each other?

Where is the love for one another?

Why can't we see beyond the barriers that

were placed around us?

Why can't we unify ourselves to protect

our very own existence?

Why do we not greet each other when

we're passing by? What are we so afraid of?

Why can't we just show a smile?

Why are we so distracted?

Why can't we pay attention?

These eyes have seen so many things

to make me question why.

Behind the Shadows

Hiding behind the Shadows never wanting to take front stage. Always in second place no intention to win the race.

Comfortable and complacent, sticking to the devil you already know. Fearing what's in front of that shadow, having no desire to grow.

Open your eyes. Wake up and smell the coffee. Get from behind and claim your place. You can do better than being number two. Come out from behind the shadows and show your face. Challenge yourself!

Game On.

New Beginnings

Yesterday is gone and can't be duplicated. Erasing it from the mind but yet it already happened.

The sun is rising the birds are singing a new day has emerged. Having the mindset to create a new beginning. It's never too late.

Decisions Decisions

Dare to take that leap of faith

to move on to the next level?

Dare to show our own true self

without feeling so uncomfortable?

You have the tools, you have the knowledge.

It has all been passed down to you.

From generation to generation,

The decision now is up to you.

Back in the Groove

Two steps forward, three steps backwards,

Where does one go from here?

What are the options, what's the next move?

Gotta get back into the groove.

Turnin' up, No turn it on down and

stay on focus stop messin' around.

The roads may be dark and lonely

but in the end there will be light.

The journey continues on, with this thing

that we call life.

Lessons Learned

You live and you learn, there's always a lesson.

Embrace the Universe's message.

Take heed to the lessons before you adjourn.

Retain all the info because knowledge has the key

to take you to where you're supposed to be.

Vibrate Higher

Speak It Now

At this nine-to-five thinking "Is this really my vision"? Knowing that there is so much more to conquer.

In a trance, thinking about my next move. There's a plethora of things to do. Escaping into a world of fantasy, hoping to bring it into reality.

It's never too late to have big dreams. Plan and execute, speak it into existence. I have big dreams, I have a vision, I speak it now into existence.

Self-Love

The moment that I saw you, I knew that I was in love. You're a beautiful sight inside and out. You are unique without a doubt. You hold yourself to the highest standards and all that I can do is stare. You are a vision of beauty, perfection at its best, an image that's supremely rare. Yes! It is I, that woman in the mirror, showering myself with love! Self-love.
Love Yourself

On My Way Up

Climbing up the mountain, reaching for the top.

With every step reminds me that there is no giving up.

Thoughts in my head, books that I've read.

Unspoken words, love that's been lost.

All tapping into my brain as I take this climb,

proving to myself that I'm not so far behind.

With my dreams and my goals, with stories

untold, when the time is right it will all unfold.

It's a tough climb but I'm almost there, anxiety

removed and having no fear. I do what I do,

I do what I can, living my best life, I am

who I am. I'll talk my talk and I'll walk my walk,

climbing that mountain, I'm on my way up.

Reaching to the very top and not giving up!

End of Chapter Notes

What is your motivation?
_____
_____
_____
_____
_____

Who/What inspires you?
_____
_____
_____
_____
_____

What are your expectations as you travel on your life's journey?
_____
_____
_____
_____
_____

Chapter 2

Universal Feelings

Connected to you

Our frequencies are balanced

Creating love sparks

Tranquility

The smell of the ocean,

listening to the waves,

quiet's my soul and opens up my mind

to a realm of creativity.

Pity Party

Trapped inside myself, wallowing in self-pity. Looking for a way out, I am my own worst

enemy.

Yearning for things that seem so

unrealistic keep gnawing at my brain.

Tossing and turning in bed at night,

driving myself insane.

Life is not always perfect, this moment is

only temporary. Mama said there would

be days like this, just put a bandage on it.

Time heals all wounds………

I Am

Why can't you just accept me for who I truly am?
Why do you try to change me to fit into your plan?
I'm not that type of person that joins in with the crowd.
I think and use my own mind stand tall
because I'm proud.
Proud to be an individual, heaven-sent uniquely made.
Someone who doesn't need acceptance or join in on the
charade.
Forgive me if I choose to walk my own path alone.
I'll make choices for myself and decide things on my own.
So please just hear me and try not to take this personally.
It's just that I am who I am, I'm an anomaly.

Nothing Left to Say

It's not that I'm avoiding you, I have nothing left to say. As time goes on, I'm finding that our lives are not the same. Trivial things that once were so important mean nothing now to me. I live a life of truth, substance and integrity.

No more fake conversations, chatting about things that do not matter. No more procrastinating waiting for someone else to save us. Waiting for elected officials to decide our fate in life. Having no desire to think and make decisions on our own.

We want different things from our lives, our directions have totally changed. My path is moving forward you're stuck on yesterday. It's not that I'm avoiding you, our goals are no longer the same. I do not want to waste your time, there's just nothing left to say.

Traces of You

Traces of you surround me,

From a distance I can hear our song.

Your scent has whisked right past me.

Your aura is very strong.

I walk alone now on this earth feeling that

you're not far behind.

The traces that have surrounded me are

of the memories when you were once

mine.

I'm Not Alone

Capturing every moment,

Listening to every word.

Feeling your vibrations

Entering into my soul.

Ignites a spark inside me

To let me know that I am not alone.

The Great Escape

Breaking away from these perilous times.

On a magical, mystical, musical high.

Escaping into my world of music.

Freeing my mind from all sorts of confusion.

Tuned into every melody, listening to the harmonies.

Mind, body and spirit on a journey.

Drifting into a place that takes my soul to another

dimension.

Where some won't have the least comprehension.

The language is universal, no need for a rehearsal.

My getaway is music. Free to be……..

Anticipation

Patiently waiting for that day.

You Take My Breath Away.

The Emptiness will be fulfilled,

My mind will be at ease.

With peace, joy and happiness.

With love unconditionally.

Fast forward to that moment, the reunion

Is so intense.

Eyes open wide to find that it was all

Just a dream.

Free

Run wild and set yourself free, there's so much of this world to see.

Remove yourself from your comfort space, be open to the gift of life and embrace.

Open up your mind, inhale and then breathe a breath of fresh air you will feel so relieved.

Take in Mother Nature's imagery of delight. It's available to you every morning, noon and night.

There's so much to do and plenty to see while traveling this road of infinity. Use all of your senses, take it all in.

You have only one life so let the journey begin.

Set yourself free with no worries or strife. Inhale then exhale and live your best life.

End of Chapter Notes

How do you manifest your feelings?

_____
_____
_____
_____
_____
_____
_____
_____
_____
_____
_____
_____

Chapter 3

Power of Love

Recklessly in love

Doing what we want to do

With no strings attached

Next Level

Where Do We Go From Here? What do we do now?

That is a question that I bring forth to you.

We've traveled many roads together, we cried

quite a few tears.

There's been so much history between us throughout so many years. But yet it seems that time stands still whenever we start to talk. And when we look into each other's eyes, there's a whirlwind full of sparks.

What's next for us, what do we do now to make the time move on

And take us to the next level right where we belong?

Roller Coaster Ride

Tell me what's on your mind. I'm no stranger to you. We've known each other long enough to speak and tell the truth. I'll listen to everything that you proposed to say. They'll be no interruptions from me oh no not today. Life is too short to leave situations unbalanced and unclear. Let's move forward, settle it now while we are both still here. I have no bad intentions, I don't have any doubt, I ask that you just open up so I know what you're talkin' about. It's like we're on this roller coaster ride that never ends. We must get off this ride somehow it's time to make amends. So come to me, I'll be right here with arms open wide, waiting for you to get off that roller coaster ride.

When the Mood is Right

Harsh words, hurt feelings

Deafening silence, created disturbances

The energy is low, our levels unbalanced

Reversing this predicament

Overcoming our plight

Clearing the air for when the mood is right

Please Wait

I tried to love you

But I didn't love myself

Hold on I'm coming

Connection

We have a connection that cannot be denied. No matter where we're place on this Earth our souls shall meet. Go on with your life, we will be just fine. We'll soon get together, it's just a matter of time.

We Are One

Focusing on our Energies,

Feeling the vibrations

Listening to the silence

Our souls connecting

Taking a deep breath

We are one

One Love

Ponder This

Touch me with your mind

Show me by your actions

Seduce me with your eyes

Then ponder over the visual

Intimacy

Caressing each other with our eyes

our bodies begin to tingle.

No words spoken, not even one touch

feeling mesmerized.

Our inner selves harmonizing with each

other, taking over, we have no control.

If this could only last forever, putting

the rest of the world on hold.

Intimacy

Stolen Moment

We embrace.

Neither of us letting go.

Hearts beating in sync.

A gentle flow.

It's time to let go.

Soft whisper in the ear.

Please Don't Let Go!

STOLEN MOMENT

The Prize

You have me with those hypnotic eyes.

You keep me with your spoken words.

Your wisdom gets me all tingly inside….

Did I happen to mention?

You make me keep a smile on my face

by showing so much affection.

Your playful ways and your gentle touch

puts me into another dimension.

Sometimes I don't know where I am

Did I happen to mention?

See you already have me with your hypnotic eyes

that puts me into a trance, I have won the prize

You!

End of Chapter Notes

What is your definition of love?
_____
_____
_____
_____
_____

Have you truly ever felt the power that love brings?
_____
_____
_____
_____
_____

How has love affected your life?
_____
_____
_____
_____
_____

Chapter 4

Mother and Daughter

Mother and daughter

A love that can't be explained

Undeniable

Mother and Daughter

As I stand In awe peeping through your door looking at a miracle that God allowed me to create.

I see innocence, strength, beauty and grace. Love, intelligence, perfection at its best. You are a part of me, I am a part of you, together we share a bond that no one else could ever view. Between us there is history and knowledge of our culture, passed down from our ancestors to allow us to continue the journey.

Those tender moments that we have shared, the times when I had to comb your hair. When you would lay across my bed to discuss a book that we both just read.

The tears and the sadness, the loss of a friend, finding the right words to heal and to mend. Not passing a test and not making the team, all the part of life but there's time to redeem. Getting words of wisdom and words of advice to dust yourself off and try again. The situation is only temporary.

Sharing the importance of being a woman and knowing respect is what we deserve. Teaching to love yourself, self-love is most important. In order to love anyone else, first you must love yourself.

This person that I see is turning into someone just like me. You're the person with your own mind who has been grounded and is set to face life…. How Divine.

So thankful to the Creator for taking Adam's rib to create woman, to bring life into the universe. Young queen you are divine and you are worthy a blessing like no other. Still looking at you with gleaming eyes even though we have been tested and tried.

We will continue on with our journey, it can only make us stronger. The road will not always be easy, but there's still so much more to discover. And as long as we have each other, we'll Journey on together, you and me, mother and daughter.

Dedication to Mother

Birthed by a queen born into royalty. Blessed to have been your daughter, thank you for the lessons that you have taught me.

You planted the seeds you watered the ground. You set the foundation for my growth. Your knowledge, wisdom, motivation and inspiration have taught me about my self-worth.

Although you are not right beside me I feel your presence as you guide me. That silent whisper in my ear, that voice that no one else can hear. It brings me comfort when I'm down it lets me know that you're around.

Even though our time together was cut short, the memories of you will stay forever in my heart. You were my first love and you will always be the one who loves me unconditionally.

You passed down the torch and I carry it now. While here on this earth I take a vow, to live my life through memories of you and your words of wisdom to help me get through.

Queen P

My dear sweet mother you are like no other. Traces of you surround me each and every day.
You may not be here physically but one thing I can see, is that you'll always be with me from here until eternity.

Worthy

Queens you are divine

Your value is infinite

Yes, you are worthy

The Journey Continues . . .

Meet the Poet

Life experiences and events have inspired me to express myself by writing this poetry book. As a novice, my intent is to motivate, uplift, and inspire others as well as allowing the reader to feel the desire to just relax and breathe.

This is a brand new experience for me. I have taken that leap of faith, and I looked forward to creating and sharing more of my creative works in the near future. I am an American writer with Caribbean roots, born and raised in New York where I currently reside with my loving family.

www.ingramcontent.com/pod-product-compliance
Lightning Source LLC
Chambersburg PA
CBHW020019050426
42450CB00005B/554